101
Ways to
Lift Your Spirits

Emilie Barnes

Artwork by Michal Sparks

HARVEST HOUSE PUBLISHERS
EUGENE, OREGON

101 Ways to Lift Your Spirits

Text Copyright © 2000 by Harvest House Publishers
Eugene, Oregon 97402

Text is adapted from *The Spirit of Loveliness* by Emilie Barnes (Harvest House Publishers, 1992).

ISBN 0-7369-0388-7

Design and production by Garborg Design Works, Minneapolis, Minnesota

To obtain more information on Emilie Barnes' More Hours in My Day seminars and tapes, please send a self-addressed, stamped business envelope to: More Hours in My Day, 2838 Rumsey Drive, Riverside, CA 92506.

All works of art reproduced in this book are from "The Creative Spark Newsletter" copyrighted by Michal Sparks and may not be reproduced without the artist's permission. For more information regarding art featured in this book, please contact: Mr. Gifford Bowne, Indigo Gate, 1 Pegasus Drive, Colts Neck, NJ 07722, (732) 577-9333.

Printed in China

00 01 02 03 04 05 06 07 08 09 / PP / 10 9 8 7 6 5 4 3 2 1

If you're like the women I meet,

you long for a beautiful life—a life where you can express the uniqueness of your God-given talents and nurture your relationships with people you love. You are hungry for a life that reflects your personality and renews your soul. A life that glows with a spirit of loveliness.

I believe this beautiful life is already there, in your heart. I hope the ideas in this little book will help it shine forth wherever you live and wherever you go.

Emilie Barnes

1 Fresh flowers are such an inexpensive way of saying welcome. You don't need a dozen roses from the florist. A bunch of daisies from the supermarket, an iris from your yard, or even a handful of dandelions from the curb can proclaim, "Love lives here."

2 Hang a bright banner by your door to say hello to everyone who comes—or try painting your door bright red!

3

If there are small children in your life,
think of ways to make your life "child-friendly"
as well as "childproof." Tuck a basket of
children's books and toys in a corner, and toss
a few throw pillows beside it to make a
welcoming place to play.

*L*ight a candle by the kitchen sink. The soft light can add a spirit of loveliness even to a tub of greasy water and a messy counter!

*W*hen you travel, plan ahead to take "home" with you. A clock radio, family pictures, or a "prayer basket" with Bible, prayer organizer, and flowers can help you make a welcoming home away from home.

6

Sometime during an evening at home, take a few minutes to go into the bedrooms and turn down the sheets. Borrow a welcoming idea from fine hotels and leave a chocolate or a little sachet on the pillow.

7

Parsley in a jar of water in the refrigerator looks inviting to those who open it. I also enjoy keeping a "bouquet" of parsley on the windowsill by the sink.

Cross-stitch or hand-letter (or commission from a talented friend) a blessing to hang by your front door on the inside, so it speaks to you, your family, and your guests as you go out into the world: "The Lord bless you and keep you; the Lord make his face shine upon you and be gracious to you; the Lord turn his face toward you and give you peace."

$\mathcal{D}$esign a "love shelf" in your home to display those little creative gifts from friends and family that mean so much but don't seem to fit anywhere.

*N*ext time you "shop the sales," buy a sheet in colors to match one of your rooms. Use it to cover a pillow or a wall—or make a drape or curtain with it. If you don't sew, wrap or tie it around the pillow or drape it on brass hooks over the window.

10

*U*se your imagination in displaying your collection of cups and saucers, bells, dolls, thimbles, and salt-and-pepper shakers. A side table, shelf, or armoire serves beautifully, but so might a printer's tray, a special basket, or a windowsill.

11

$\mathcal{D}$uring the fall, go out to a local farm and pick pumpkins for centerpieces, yard decorations, and, of course, pumpkin pie! Better yet, plant a package of seeds in July for a fall harvest.

13

*T*hrow a pretty tablecloth over your coffee table and serve hors d'oeuvres, tea, coffee, or dessert in the living room or den instead of the dining room or kitchen. Or try setting up a card table for dinner in the garden. Your family or your guests will love the change of pace.

14

*J*ust a little creative touch can make an everyday table extra special. Tie a ribbon around your napkins; add a fresh flower, a few dried flowers, or a piece of ivy.

$\mathcal{M}$ark off time on your calendar for baking bread, practicing piano, or whatever stimulates your creative juices. Creative time is just like any time; if it's not scheduled, something else will probably crowd it out.

$\mathcal{F}$or an extra-homey dinner, try using a quilt as a tablecloth. Or drape a worn-out sofa with a bright quilt to camouflage and decorate at the same time.

17

If you sing or play an instrument, offer to share the gift of your creativity with a local rest home or daycare center. You don't have to be a polished performer to share a lot of joy.

18

At dinner, place individual candles in front of the place settings. Let guests and family members light their own candles and describe something they are thankful for or the best thing that happened that day.

*T*ake advantage of a free hour to write a story for your children or grandchildren—or some other child in your life. Draw illustrations and send it as a surprise, or read it onto an audiotape for bedtime pleasure.

20 A plate or basket of fresh fruit on the nightstand adds color and fragrance to the room before it becomes a bedtime snack.

21 The small green Perrier water bottles make great bud vases. Tie a tiny bow around the neck of the bottle and fill it with flowers. Place in front of each person's plate at dinner, or take one to a friend who needs cheering up.

$\mathcal{M}$ake *creative* giving a tradition in your household. In addition to modeling creativity for your kids, provide supplies, space, instruction, and encouragement to make their own cards and gifts.

$\mathcal{S}$pray the sheets with baby powder or sweet perfume before crawling into bed. You'll enjoy a welcome sense of relaxation—as well as feeling absolutely beautiful.

Collect perfume samples and scented inserts from magazine ads to freshen your drawers or suitcases. Or try spraying your own cologne on the drawer liners to give a scent of you.

24

Next time you take a walk, pick a few flowers. Tuck them in a vase by your bed…on your husband's side.

25

To add a touch of caring and whimsy, use stickers or rubber stamps on your notes, letters, even bills. Write with colored pens, use colored paper clips, and tuck in sprinkles of confetti for a festive message.

Take a hint from great-grandmother:
Dab a bit of vanilla behind your ears for a tasty fragrance.

$\mathcal{S}$tring one-inch white eyelet along the edge of your closet shelf. Attach it with thumbtacks, a hot glue gun, or a heavy-duty stapler for a great feminine look.

28

$\mathcal{I}$f you wear a suit to the office, try the old-fashioned custom of wearing a rosebud or a tiny bunch of violets on your lapel. Ask your local florist about tiny holders that can keep your flower fresh.

29

Cover shoeboxes with floral wrapping paper or wallpaper for your shoes. They look great on the floor or shelf. (Use spray adhesive, staples, or a hot glue gun.)

*T*ake an afternoon off to play "dress up" with a little girl in your life. Deck yourselves out in your finery, help her put on a little makeup and jewelry, and visit a local tea room for ice cream or a muffin.

*D*o you remember finding a smooth stone and loving the cool touch? Find another one. As you hold it in your hand, thank God for the strong and lovely gift of your femininity.

Get inspired by reading the story of a great woman of the past or present. Some ideas: Margaret of Cortona, Elizabeth Fry, Dolly Madison, Lottie Moon, Amy Carmichael, Elisabeth Elliot, Ruth Bell Graham, Mother Teresa.

In the spring, take a child (or yourself) for a "senses walk." Smell the roses, the orange blossoms, the sweet peas; see how many different fragrances you can detect. Gently pull the stamen from a honeysuckle blossom and taste the nectar. Close your eyes and listen for different sounds— birds, woodpecker, train, foghorn, airplane, saw, hammer, water.

For an investment in the future, plant a tree! If you don't have a yard, think about making a "green" donation to your church grounds or even a local school.

In a kitchen, where so many hours are spent, one spray of fragrant lilac blossoms in a child's battered mug can brighten the day.

37

Your front door can always say "welcome" with a May basket, a fall arrangement of Indian corn, or a green wreath for Christmas.

38

If the green or yellow or bittersweet pots you find in a garden shop don't match your pale pink (or bright-red) window, just buy white plastic pots and a can of spray paint. In just a few minutes you can have pots to fit your decor.

$\mathcal{T}$ry using plants as architectural helps—a group of tall plants to divide a room, for instance, or a combination of potted and hanging plants to partially screen a window.

40

*I*n the kitchen window, a row of herb plants that you can grow from seed or buy in three-inch pots will not only be decorative, but will add distinctive flavor to gourmet dishes.

41

⊛n the sun porch, fill an attractive wheeled cart with blooming fibrous begonias. Brighten the dining room with an indoor window box of impatiens.

*A*re you on a seed catalog list? Send for every catalog you read about. It's an easy way to learn the names of flowers and a great opportunity to see them in color.

If time or space prohibit a full garden, plant tomatoes and strawberries in a barrel or other large container. You'll be surprised at the yield from just a few plants.

43

$\star$rder ladybugs from a gardening catalog or nursery and let children help release them around garden or yard. Ladybugs are God's way of keeping harmful bugs under control—and kids love to help them "fly away home."

44

Try companion planting.
Some flowers such as marigolds act as natural
insect repellants to protect your crops.

*M*ake your kitchen a place that says "Welcome." A bowl of freshly washed lemons is a great way to say "Hello!"

*F*or a low-maintenance, high-pleasure garden, scatter a packet of wildflower seeds. If you wait until the seed heads are ripe in the summer before mowing it down, it will reseed itself year after year.

Did you ever grow a sweet-potato garden as a child? Get a quart-sized jar and a sweet potato, and try it again. (All you have to do is stick the potato in water and wait.) Better yet, share the fun of growing a potato with your favorite child.

*M*ake the inside of your refrigerator a feast for the eye. Use see-through containers for fruit. Even a small bowl of flowers can bless the eye of anyone looking for a snack.

49

*S*erve your butter in a white pottery crock. Whip it with an equal amount of olive oil to stretch the butter. It will fluff up beautifully.

50

51

Freeze grapes and roll them in granulated sugar. Store in a glass bowl or on a pretty plate and toss in a salad or use as a garnish.

52

For a creative surprise, serve breakfast for dinner. Our family loves waffles with toppings of fruit, nuts, coconut, raisins, jams, maple syrup, and yogurt.

$\mathcal{S}$tore foods in ways that allow them to be decorative as well as useful. Display fruit in a basket or special bowl on the kitchen table or drainboard. Stack potatoes and onions in a basket and use it to enliven an out-of-the way corner of your counter or floor.

Next time you make buttered toast, sprinkle on some cinnamon and sugar. An old idea, but when was the last time you did it?

Add one-half teaspoon ground cinnamon and a pinch of ground cloves to your coffee grounds next time you brew. Drink out of your favorite cup and saucer and enjoy the fresh flavor and smell.

56 On a slow afternoon, put on soft music and browse through your favorite recipe book for ideas and inspiration.

57 Hang a basket or two—or thirty!—from the ceiling beam or over a wall in the kitchen or breakfast room.

58

Dejunk your kitchen fifteen minutes at a time. The room will look more spacious and you'll be more inspired to spend time there.

59

Help a child plant some seeds in a small container and place it in your kitchen window to sprout.

60

Instead of putting the catsup bottle on the table, serve catsup in a little crock with a spoon.

Instead of buying regular applesauce, buy apples. A bowl of homemade applesauce with a sprinkle of cinnamon is a healthful, easy-to-make snack or dessert.

Just once during the summer, turn dinner into celebration time by serving sundaes or banana splits for your main meal. It's a lot less fattening than dinner *plus* banana splits, and the one time won't ruin anyone's health.

63

Rearrange your bedroom furniture so that the first thing you see as you enter is the bed. Rejoice in the sense of welcome.

64

A made-up bed is always more welcoming and relaxing than a tangle of sheets. Make a rule in your house that the last one out of the bed makes it up.

Clutter wearies the spirit and fights against serenity. At the very least, take fifteen minutes to dejunk the room where you spend your quiet time.

*R*ead Ecclesiastes 3—the whole chapter. List from that chapter what time in life it is for you now. What percentage of your life is available for inward pursuits?

*K*eep a Bible, writing paper, and a pen on your bedside table for spiritual food during still moments. If you run a lot of errands, keep a Bible or an inspirational book in your car.

Shortly before your family comes home, take a minute to create a serene atmosphere. Clear the clutter in the living room or entry hall, light candles, put on soft music. And call a moratorium on problems and "discussions" for the next thirty minutes. If you live alone, give yourself half an hour of rest before tackling the evening chores.

*T*ry setting aside a "quiet corner" at home with books, comfortable cushions, warm light. Make a family agreement to make stillness a priority for anyone in that place.

*D*on't be afraid to take time out for quiet when things get too much. Unless your children are very small, set a timer for fifteen minutes and disappear into bedroom or bathroom. Read your Bible or simply lie still and *be*.

71

*C*hildren need stillness, too. Try to make sure that every child in your home has a place where he or she can go to get away from the bustle and just be quiet.

72

*I*f you work outside the home, try setting aside your lunch hour as a time for stillness. Take a walk somewhere quiet and lovely. Drive to a park or find a quiet corner in a restaurant—or go home. Read, pray, and return to your job refreshed.

Frame a card with your favorite Scripture verse and hang the little picture next to your desk or sink. When you need a break, ponder it.

Explore one of the classic books that have lifted the faith of so many believers over the years. Oswald Chambers' *My Utmost for His Highest*, Hannah Whitehall Smith's *The Christian's Secret of a Happy Life*, or any of C.S. Lewis' books are wonderful places to start.

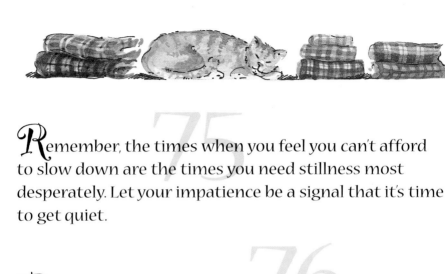

Remember, the times when you feel you can't afford to slow down are the times you need stillness most desperately. Let your impatience be a signal that it's time to get quiet.

Frame a family photo and put it in the bathroom. Pray each morning for your family as you brush your teeth, do your makeup, or style your hair.

$\mathcal{A}$sk an acquaintance at church to be your prayer partner for a set period of time. Meet or call each other once a day to share concerns and pray together. Or exercise body and spirit and pray together as you take a walk.

$\mathcal{B}$e on the lookout for ways to serve others. This could mean something as simple as helping in the church nursery or as complex as volunteering to organize an emergency food pantry at your church.

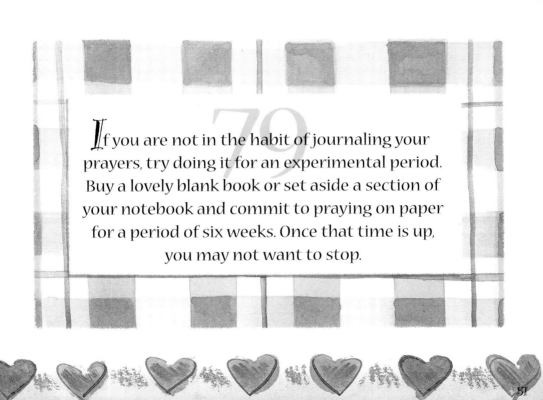

79

If you are not in the habit of journaling your prayers, try doing it for an experimental period. Buy a lovely blank book or set aside a section of your notebook and commit to praying on paper for a period of six weeks. Once that time is up, you may not want to stop.

*L*ook for ways to turn your everyday activities into occasions for prayer and thanksgiving. As you scrub the toilets or hose down the front stairs, ask God to use those mundane tasks to His glory. As you jog or ride your exercise bike, thank God for the gift of your body and the wonderful way you are made, no matter what your particular shape!

$\mathcal{Y}$ou don't have to be a little girl to love a tea party!
I love to serve my afternoon guests fragrant
cinnamon tea, poured into their choice from my
cup and saucer collection, and my wonderful,
healthful oatmeal cookies.

$\mathcal{T}$ry taking your hospitality on the road. Fill a
basket with food and take it to someone who needs
encouragement.

*D*o you know your neighbors? Build a sense of brotherhood in your area by inviting neighbors over for dinner or a snack. Or for a fun event, host a neighborhood barbecue.

*E*ven if you don't have children, keep a supply of cookies and Popsicles in your freezer and invite neighborhood children over regularly to talk and play.

A favorite event at our house is a waffle-bar brunch or tea. I serve delicate multigrain waffles with bowls of fresh strawberries, grated coconut, raisins, slivered almonds, real whipping cream, vanilla yogurt, and real maple syrup from Vermont.

86

*P*lace a tiny gift by your dinner guests' plates—a small address book, a pen, nail clippers, a hankie, a powder puff, a pot holder tied with a bow, a dishtowel or dishcloth, or an autographed book. Everyone loves a present.

87

*T*ry serving a shift or two in your local soup kitchen or food bank. Better still, volunteer on a regular basis.

*I*nvest in extra pillows, blankets, and other bedding for overnight guests, and store them in pillowcases to keep them fresh and dust-free.

*I*f your budget is slim, try hosting a potluck or a theme dinner to which every guest is invited to bring a dish. Or invite six or eight friends to start a "supper club" with you, meeting each month in a different home and contributing dishes to a different menu.

What aspect of your home or apartment do you enjoy most—the view, the quiet, the yard? Let that aspect be the focus of your hospitality. Share the aspects of your life that bring you pleasure.

Try putting an overnight guest in your child's room for the night and give your child the "privilege" of camping out in the living room. The result: an adventure for your child and welcome privacy for your guest.

91

92

Place photos of you with your guest on the bedside table in the guest room.

*M*ake laughter a tradition in your family. Tell jokes, clip cartoons, share funny stories about things that happened to you during the day. And don't overlook opportunities to poke fun at yourself when you make a mistake. Through your example, kids can learn not to take themselves too seriously.

*C*elebrate your memories. Choose one day a year to gather and look through photo albums, show slides, and watch home videos.

95

ven if guests elect to stay in a nearby motel, you can extend hospitality with a few special touches. Have a floral arrangement sent to their room. Or leave a basket of homemade muffins at the desk for their arrival.

$\mathcal{W}$rite mom and/or dad—or whoever was responsible for raising you—a letter about your favorite memories and your favorite traditions your family celebrated when you were a child. Be sure to say thank you!

96

$\mathcal{L}$et down your hair and play games like tag and hide-and-seek as a whole family. Modify the rules, if you have to, so that all ages can join in—and remember to have fun.

97

One of the best ways to celebrate God's gifts is to share them. Several times a year create a "Love Basket" filled with food for a needy family or the homeless. Or try spending part of your holidays helping out at a local rescue mission.

Celebrate your friendships with other women by throwing an "all girls" party. I love to do this in the spring with tea, fresh flowers, and a lovely brunch.

*M*ark the beginning of a new phase of your life—a marriage, a new baby, even a new house—by starting a tradition. One couple I know has their photo taken every year on their anniversary. Their collection now includes formal shots, household portraits, and one quickie snap taken by strangers on a roadside campground.

100

*K*eep a list of blessings in your life. Go over the list each morning and remember that you have reason to celebrate every day.

101